OXFORD

Revising AQA GCSE English

AQA

Peter Buckroyd

Specification **A**

AQA GCSE English

Foundation and Higher Tiers

OXFORD

UNIVERSITY PRESS

Great Clarendon Street, Oxford OX2 6DP

Oxford University Press is a department of the University of Oxford.
It furthers the University's objective of excellence in research, scholarship,
and education by publishing worldwide in

Oxford New York

Auckland Bangkok Buenos Aires Cape Town Chennai
Dar es Salaam Delhi Hong Kong Istanbul Karachi Kolkata
Kuala Lumpur Madrid Melbourne Mexico City Mumbai Nairobi
São Paulo Shanghai Taipei Tokyo Toronto

Oxford is a registered trade mark of Oxford University Press
in the UK and in certain other countries

© Peter Buckroyd 2003

British Library Cataloguing in Publication Data

Data available

ISBN 0 19 831889 8

1 3 5 7 9 10 8 6 4 2

Typeset and assembled by Blenheim Colour Ltd, Eynsham, Oxford

Printed in Italy by Rotolito Lombardo

For Ollie, my inspiration for this book

Acknowledgements

We are grateful for permission to reproduce the following copyright material:

Atlantic Syndication: Extract from 'Is this man really the very model of modern masculinity?' first published in *The Daily Mail* 03.02.03.

Express Newspaper: Extract from 'Refugees must get working' first published in *Daily Express* 05.02.03; Extract from 'All hail my hero Paula says Haile' by John Wragg first published in *Daily Express* 05.02.03; accompanying photograph of Paula Radcliffe by Dan Chung, 2002, reprinted by permission of Reuters News Picture Service.

Mirror Syndication: Extract from 'Bad Samaritan' first published in *Daily Mirror* 03.02.02.

N I Syndication: Advert for half price flights in association with American Airlines first published in *The Times* 23.01.03, copyright © News International Newspapers Limited, London 2003; extract from 'Archbishop backs tories on detention' by David Charter first published in *The Times* 03.02.03, copyright © News International Newspapers Ltd, London 2003; extract from 'His Duty' first published in *The Sun* 03.02.03, copyright © News International Newspapers Limited, London 2003; and extract from 'MacArthur keeps record in sights' by Keith Wheatley, copyright © Keith Wheatley/News International Newspapers Limited 2003; accompanying photograph of Ellen MacArthur by Charles Platiau, 2002, reprinted by permission of Reuters News Picture Service.

Vauxhall Motors Ltd: Media advertisement for Vauxhall Motors.

CONTENTS

Welcome to *Revising AQA GCSE English* for *Specification A*.

This book is designed to help you to revise effectively for your two English examinations. Some people say that they can't do much revision for English because only a quarter of the exam is on texts they have studied. Of course you can revise the poems you have studied for Paper 2, but you can also brush up the skills which will be tested in both exams.

This book therefore concentrates on skills. It takes you back to the Assessment Objectives and explains what each of them means in terms of what you need to think about and what skills you need to show when you write.

You can do a lot to prepare for your response to unseen non-fiction texts and also for the two pieces of writing that you are tested on. This book will take you through each kind of writing in turn, looking at some of the most common features of each type and the forms that you are most frequently asked to write in. There are also some tips about planning and checking, both of which are very important if you are going to gain as many marks as you possibly can. I have also included some examples of students' work at different grades to help you to see how the mark schemes work and what you can do to try to improve your grade.

The non-fiction texts included in this book are at various levels – some are more suitable for Foundation tier candidates, others for Higher tier. At this stage, you should focus on the texts you find most interesting, but a rough guide to level would be as follows:

Foundation – 'Bad Samaritan', 'Refugees must get working', 'His duty' (all p.10), 'Is this man …' (p.13), 'All hail my hero …' (p.17)

Higher – 'Archbishop backs Tories …' (p.11), 'MacArthur keeps record in sights' (p.16).

Similarly, bullets are used as part of the exam-style questions to offer support where needed – but, of course, don't feel you have to use them!

The skills needed for writing about the poems from different cultures and traditions are also covered, together with some advice about how to compare poems effectively. There are also some examples of students' work, with comments from an examiner.

I hope you will enjoy tackling some of the tasks I have included. The best advice I can give you is to plan your revision schedule carefully and to get a good night's sleep before each exam so that you can think clearly and freshly about the questions which you are faced with.

I hope it all goes well for you.

Peter Buckroyd

Introduction

In order to revise effectively for this exam, you don't have to look just at what you have done in your English classes or at the extracts in this book. In fact, one of the most important ways that you can practise your skills for this part of the exam is by reading and thinking about absolutely any written material that you come across.

If you don't usually get a newspaper, get one while you are revising because it will give you lots of practice in identifying and commenting on presentational devices. It doesn't matter which newspaper you choose, but it would be good to look at different papers on different days. Read the stories and articles about things which interest you, but also have a look at the advertisements. Notice the various styles of writing that are used and think about their effects.

Assessment Objectives and how to meet them

These are the Assessment Objectives that are tested in this part of the exam, the first section of Paper 1:

❏ Read, with insight and engagement, making appropriate references to texts and developing and sustaining interpretations of them.

❏ Distinguish between fact and opinion and evaluate how information is presented.

❏ Follow an argument, identifying implications and recognizing inconsistencies.

❏ Select material appropriate to their purpose, collate material from different sources, and make cross references.

❏ Understand and evaluate how writers use linguistic, structural and presentational devices to achieve their effects, and comment on the ways language varies and changes.

I am going to split these Assessment Objectives up into their different parts to show you exactly what they mean and what you need to do to meet them.

Tip! *You won't get questions on all of these but you don't know which the examiners will choose to test you. You need to be prepared to answer on any of them.*

Read with insight and engagement, making appropriate references to texts and developing and sustaining interpretations of them.

Read with insight and engagement

- Try to understand and follow what is being said.
- Try to get on the writer's wavelength.

Make appropriate references to texts

- Use details from the text to support what you have to say.
- Scan the text to make sure you've got a range of appropriate material with which to answer the question.
- Make sure that everything you choose is relevant to the question.

Develop and sustain interpretations of them

- Link your points together.
- Make sure that each follows the previous one effectively.
- Try to organize your points in the best order so that the reader can follow your ideas.

Distinguish between fact and opinion and evaluate how information is presented.

Distinguish between fact and opinion

- If you are asked about this, there will be several facts and several opinions to be found.
- Choose what seem to you to be most obviously facts.
- Don't choose those which are opinions disguised as facts (false facts).
- Opinions will not have any factual evidence to support them.

Evaluate how information is presented

- Make a list of the different devices used to present information.
- Comment on how effective these are in achieving their purpose.
- Express your opinion of the effectiveness of how the information is presented.
- Remember that just because the text is printed in the exam it doesn't mean that it is necessarily good or effective. It might have been chosen for you to evaluate by pointing out good things and/or weaknesses.

Follow an argument, identifying implications and recognizing inconsistencies.

Follow an argument
- Find the main point (the 'thesis') of the writing.
- Then identify the subsidiary points.
- Look carefully at the order in which the points, or the argument, are presented and see if you can comment on it.
- Make sure you don't copy out chunks of the passage.
- Select your material to identify the argument and outline its shape and its stages.

Identify implications
- Language is often used to influence you or to imply things.
- Work out the tone of the text.
- Work out what is conveyed to you without telling you directly.
- Sometimes the writer's language might hint at broader ideas or attitudes. Think about what he or she might be hinting at.

Recognize inconsistencies
- These could be:
  - contradictions within the text
  - differences in the way information and ideas are presented in two different texts
  - weaknesses in part of the argument which undermine the effectiveness of the argument as a whole
  - a contradiction between the article and the headline
  - lack of agreement between the writing and the illustrations.

Select material appropriate to their purpose, collate material from different sources, and make cross references.

Select material appropriate to purpose
- This usually means 'answer the question'.
- Trawl through the text in order to find a range of relevant material.
- Look for a range of different points to make rather than find several examples of the same point.

Collate material from different sources
- Pick out things from more than one text.
- This will enable you to make comparisons.
- 'Collate' means 'put together'.

Make cross references
- This means 'compare'.
- Choose your material carefully to make sure that you can find a range of points of similarity and difference.
- Sometimes there may be more points of difference than of similarity, so you could organize what you have to say round a series of differences. 'Compare' doesn't mean that you always have to find things that are similar.

Understand and evaluate how writers use linguistic, structural and presentational devices to achieve their effects, and comment on the ways language varies and changes.

Understand and evaluate how writers use linguistic devices to achieve their effects

- Identify these devices. These might be: formal and informal register, alliteration, metaphor, simile, repetition, groups of three, rhetorical questions, minor sentences, modifiers, emotive language, transactional language, imperatives, modal verbs.
- Comment on any features of language that you can find.
- Concentrate on explaining how the writers use the devices, i.e. think about their purpose and how effective they are.

Structural devices

- Identify these devices. These might be: topic sentences, connectives, paragraphs, discourse features, headlines, sub-headings.
- Comment on any features of structure that you can find.
- Concentrate your energies on explaining how the writers use these devices, i.e. think about their purpose and how effective they are.

Presentational devices

- Identify the devices. These might be: headlines, bold print, italics, font size, straplines, bylines, pictures, photographs, line drawings, graphs, the angle and position of the writing, the angle and position of the illustrations, any white space, bullet points, underlining, cross-heads, captions, logos, standfirst.
- Comment on any features of presentation that you can find.
- Concentrate your energies on explaining how the writers use these devices, i.e. think about their purpose and how effective they are.

Comment on the ways language varies and changes

- This might take the form of: narrative, direct speech, regional variation, class variation, outdated language (archaism), features of language characteristic of its date.
- Concentrate on explaining the purpose and effect of these aspects of language variation and change.

Grid for comparing texts

In at least one of the exam questions you will be asked to compare texts, so it's important to prepare for this during your revision. One way of structuring the comparison for revision is to use the Assessment Objectives.

Use the chart on page 9 to make notes on some of the following media texts (or any other non-fiction texts that you use for revision).

Features to consider	Text 1	Text 2
What is the medium? \n\n Evidence		
What is the purpose? \n\n Evidence		
Who is the audience? \n\n Evidence		
What is the main argument (or point)?		
How is this developed (or elaborated)?		
What presentational devices are used? \n\n Effects created		
What structural devices are used? \n\n Effects created		
What linguistic devices are used? \n\n Effects created		
Which is the more successful? \n\n Why?		

Revision tasks

Here are some materials for you to practise on. They are not designed to be trial exams. They are meant to allow you to focus on the Assessment Objectives and to practise your skills.

Revision task 1

Look at these four reports of the same story from different newspapers:

- a leader from the *Daily Mirror*
- a leader from the *Daily Express*
- a leader from *The Sun*
- an article on the front page of *The Times*.

Article 1

Bad Samaritan

The views of the new Archbishop of Canterbury on asylum seekers are remarkably unChristian.

Rowan Williams sees nothing wrong with locking them up while they are investigated in case some are terrorists.

The proportion of asylum seekers who are a threat is small. They must be rooted out and detained, naturally.

But it would be scandalous to smear those genuinely fleeing terror in their own countries as if they were a threat.

The problem of asylum seekers, refugees and immigration generally is a huge and vital one – though it is made much worse by newspapers exploiting the situation.

An intelligent and serious debate is needed. And the Archbishop of Canterbury should be playing a crucial role in it.

Besides, where does he propose locking up all those asylum seekers?

Lambeth Palace?

▲ From the *Daily Mirror*, 3rd February 2003

Article 2

Refugees must get working

None of the 1,000 immigrants who entered Britain with the Government's blessing when the Sangatte refugee camp in France was closed has got jobs. Instead, they will soon be able to claim state handouts.

The closure of Sangatte was supposed to relieve the pressure of illegal immigrants on these shores. Instead, it has resulted in an easy ride into this country for individuals who appear to want nothing more than to leech off the state. Home Secretary David Blunkett must make sure these immigrants, who have been given every chance to get a job, start to pay their own way.

▲ From the *Daily Express*, 3rd February 2003

Article 3

His duty

THE new Archbishop of Canterbury started his job with a whimper.

Until yesterday, that is.

Suddenly Dr Rowan Williams emerges not as a wishy-washy, hand-wringing liberal but as a man in touch with reality.

He backs The Sun's campaign on asylum seekers saying it is "perfectly reasonable" to lock them up while their claims are checked out.

In the wake of the tragic death of DC Stephen Oake, Dr Williams demands that the Government be "absolutely serious about security."

We applaud the Archbishop's boldness.

It would have been so easy for him to hide behind a "turn the other cheek" attitude.

But like the Muslim leaders who have supported our views, he knows his duty is to his people.

From *The Sun*, 3rd February 2003 ▶

Article 4

Archbishop backs Tories on detention of refugees

By David Carter
Chief Political Correspondent

THE TORIES last night seized on comments by the Archbishop of Canterbury backing their call for every asylum-seeker to be security vetted while under lock and key.

Dr Rowan Williams said that it would be "perfectly reasonable" for those hoping to stay in Britain to be kept in secure accommodation while their cases were being considered.

The Archbishop's intervention comes during a period of intense national debate over asylum-seekers and after an appeal for calm by David Blunkett, the Home Secretary, who gave a warning that the hysteria could boil over into violence.

Tony Blair said last week that Britain could withdraw from international treaties so it could deport failed asylum-seekers if present policies do not stem the flow of 100,000 a year while the Tories insisted that all new arrivals should not be released until they pass security checks. Dr Williams was criticised by a range of refugee and civil liberty groups but Mr Blunkett was said to be "relaxed" about his comments.

The Home Secretary may be keen to avoid another public row with Dr Williams after they tangled a month ago over the Archbishop's attack on the lack of ethical values in politics.

However, Oliver Letwin, the Shadow Home Secretary, said; "When an Archbishop noted for his liberal views agrees with a Conservative policy that for the safety of the public at a time of national emergency the security vetting of asylum-seekers should take place in secure accommodation, who can any longer doubt that this is in the national interest?

"The Archbishop's welcome comments give the lie to anybody that suggests that the Conservative position is extreme or inhumane. It is time for David Blunkett and Tony Blair to think again – and fast."

From *The Times,* 3rd February 2003

1   Pick out the facts that you can find in each of these articles.

2   Comment on the balance of fact and opinion in each of the articles and say what effects you think are achieved by these combinations.

3   Which of the four seems to you to be the most balanced? Give your evidence and explain why you think this is.

4   What can you deduce about the attitudes and biases expressed in each of these articles? Give your evidence by looking closely at the language.

5   For each article, express in one sentence what you think is the main point being made.

6   Compare and contrast the language in the leader from *The Sun* and the leader from the *Daily Mirror.* What does the language show you about the purpose of these articles? What effect does it have on you, the reader, and why?

7   Look at the presentational devices in each of the articles and explain what you think their purposes and effects are.

Revision task 2

Read the following article about David Beckham.

1   Summarize the main findings of the research done by Dr Parker and Professor Ellis Cashmore.

2   Highlight the facts that are included in this article.

3   What do the writers achieve by including this amount of fact compared to that of opinion in the article?

4   What effects are achieved by the presentation of the article? Look particularly at the picture, the layout, the headlines.

5   What, according to the article, is 'a modern man'? Give your evidence fully.

Notes

David Beckham is changing male behaviour, say experts

Is this man really the very model of modern masculinity?

NO ONE would question his status among soccer fans throughout the world.

But David Beckham is today being credited by academics with single-handedly transforming male behaviour and attitudes on a global scale.

The England captain, who changes his hairstyle more often than some men change their socks, strikes a chord with everyone between the ages of five and 60, says a university study.

Research into the effects of 27-year-old Beckham's worldwide fame claims his much-derided, idiosyncratic style and approach to life have helped transform men's attitudes to sex, love, babies and even homosexuality.

The study singles out the Manchester United midfielder's love of fashion and shopping as one way in which the sarong-wearing star – whose earnings topped £15 million last year – is redefining the model of a modern man.

'Beckham is not only a strong role model.

'He has helped to break masculine codes by defying various manly expectations such as what clothes men are allowed to wear,' said Warwick University sociology professor Dr Andrew Parker, co-author of the study.

'He is managing to single-handedly change male behaviour globally and for the better.'

Beckham's wife Victoria, the former Posh Spice, has come in for equal derision from some quarters – not to mention taunts of an even more personal nature from the terraces.

Yet Beckham has never shied away from displaying or publicly declaring his dedication to her and their sons – Brooklyn, three, and five-month-old Romeo – and this only adds to his status as a beacon of inspiration, the study says.

And while maintaining an aura of laddishness by the very fact of being a footballer and a national hero, Beckham transcends the game's boorish, stereotyped image.

'Every mother's favourite'

'Although he is still "one of the lads" we never see him as a drinker,' adds Dr Parker.

'Instead he appears to prioritise family time, which is unusual in the world of football which is predominantly seen as a very masculine sport.'

Dr Parker and his co-author Professor Ellis Cashmore, of Staffordshire University, will unveil their findings at a conference this week.

Their research is entitled One David Beckham: Celebrity, Masculinity and the Soccerati. The study describes the player as both a 'new man' and a 'new lad' or 'dad lad'.

But the authors say he also shows worthy traits of the 'old industrial man', such as loyalty, stoicism and a determination to be the breadwinner.

Beckham symbolises the breakdown of male stereotypes by showing an interest in ballet and fashion, publicly confessing his love for his wife and even daring to acknowledge his large gay following, say the academics.

'Despite his high profile and ridicule he risks, Beckham stands resolute: bucking the "macho" trend, setting his own agenda, showing support for his wife, playing the perfect father, remaining every mother's favourite – while at the same time, on the field, displaying the spirit and patriotism of a national ambassador,' they write.

Beckham's public endorsements of Marks & Spencer and Vodafone also reflect his 'family man' ideals, says Dr Parker.

'English professional soccer may not modify its masculine profile as a direct result of David Beckham,' say the authors, 'but his popular kudos could stimulate change in terms of masculine norms and expectations both inside and outside of sport – both inside and outside of sporting locales in the years to come.'

The research is due for publication in the Sociology of Sport Journal later this year.

From the *Daily Mail*, 3rd February 2003

Revision task 3

Look at the following two advertisements.

Advert 1

0% FINANCE FOR 3 YEARS

Corsa SXi £8,995

- 1.2i 16v • Sports front seats • CD player
- Alloy-effect interior features • 15-inch alloy wheels
- 3 years' warranty and AA cover**

PLUS 1 YEAR'S FREE INSURANCE*

Astra SXi £11,995

- 1.6i 16v • Air conditioning • CD player
- Sports front seats • Sports suspension
- 16-inch alloy wheels
- 3 years' warranty and AA cover**

Vectra SXi £15,990

- 2.2i 16v • Air conditioning • Cruise control
- Sports front seats • ABS • Traction control
- CD player • 16-inch alloy wheels
- 3 years' warranty and AA cover**

2003 is our centenary so we've got a great deal to celebrate.
Buy one of these models before March 31st and we'll give you 3 years' 0% finance. Now that's worth celebrating.

Call 0845 600 1500 now or visit www.vauxhall.co.uk

100 YEARS OF VAUXHALL. A GREAT DEAL TO CELEBRATE.

VAUXHALL
A Century in Motion

Advert 2

HALF PRICE FLIGHTS

BOOK YOUR SEATS FOR 24 GREAT DESTINATIONS TODAY

Fly First or Business Class to 30 transatlantic destinations or take up a 2 for 1 offer on Economy tickets to the same locations. Los Angeles, Mexico City, Miami. New Orleans. Orlando and St Louis are available to book from today.

HOW TO BOOK

If you have collected eight passwords, including two from *The Sunday Times*, you can start booking your flights for the first 24 destinations from the list, right. The last six destinations will be released tomorrow. Passwords will appear until this Sunday and at least two of the ones you use must come from *The Sunday Times*. Once you have all eight, call the number below by January 31, quote your passwords and book your seats. Please note: Economy fares quoted are for two people.

You can fly, from Gatwick or Heathrow, as late as May 31 and, if necessary, take advantage of special £45 return transfers from Aberdeen, Dublin, Edinburgh, Glasgow, Inverness, Manchester, Newcastle and Newquay. For special deals on hotels and travel insurance, please call 0871 222 1256.

E-mail flightofferhelp@timesonline.co.uk with any queries.

BOOKING LINE:

0845 606 0462

Or visit www.timesonline.co.uk/travel for details of an alternative booking procedure.

WHAT'S IMPORTANT
THE TIMES
AmericanAirlines®

PASSWORD 13: CASINO

THE SPECIAL FARES*

Destination	First class	Business	Economy	
Outward flights start from London Heathrow/Gatwick			Economy fares are for two people	
			Until April 30	*May*
New York	£3,247	£1,968	£268	£376
Raleigh/Durham	£3,299	£2,102	£268	£400
San Diego	£3,429	£3,015	£341	£463
Tampa	£3,792	£2,083	£351	£518
Toronto	£3,932	£2,168	£359	£449
San Juan, PR	£2,677	£1,885	£671	£627
Atlanta	£3,299	£2,127	£268	£376
Boston	£3,247	£1,968	£268	£376
Memphis	£3,430	£2,399	£349	£458
Nashville	£3,430	£2,370	£402	£511
Seattle	£3,792	£3,015	£341	£463
Washington DC	£3,299	£2,063	£268	£376
Chicago	£3,456	£2,469	£310	£432
Dallas	£3,429	£2,540	£310	£432
Philadelphia	£3,930	£1,947	£268	£376
Phoenix	£3,758	£3,015	£341	£463
San Francisco	£3,792	£3,015	£310	£432
Buenos Aires	£4,214	£2,867	£675	£675
Orlando	£3,299	£2,083	£351	£518
Los Angeles	£3,792	£3,015	£310	£432
Miami	£3,427	£2,126	£334	£498
Mexico City	£2,667	£1,732	£542	£535
New Orleans	£3,100	£2,744	£370	£492
St Louis	£3,390	£2,017	£335	£468
Denver	£4,490	£2,632	£413	£463
Las Vegas	£3,758	£3,130	£361	£514
Rio de Janeiro	£3,793	£2,476	£660	£665
Barbados	£3,137	£1,886	£627	£548
Honolulu	£4,451	£3,917	£699	£824
Salt Lake City	£4,215	£2,890	£557	£608

(left margin on last six rows: BOOK FROM TOMORROW)

*Prices do not include taxes. Taxes vary up to £62 per person travelling Economy and up to £72 per person for First and Business.

---

1   What is the purpose of each of these advertisements?

2   What kind of reader do you think each is aimed at? Give your reasons by supporting your comments with detail from the adverts.

3   Compare and contrast the two advertisements in terms of:
    ◆ their overall look and layout
    ◆ the illustrations
    ◆ the amount and type of writing
    ◆ the language and vocabulary
    ◆ the use of particular features commonly used in advertisements.

4   Which would be more likely to get you to part with your money, if you had any, and why?

Revision task 4

Read these two articles, which report and celebrate sporting achievements.

Article 1

MacArthur keeps record in sights

The first few days at sea took their toll on crew and boat, but Kingfisher2 is gaining on world record time in the Jules Verne trophy, writes **Keith Wheatley**

MacArthur: back on course

ELLEN MacARTHUR and the crew of Kingfisher2 are streaking towards the equator on day four of their Jules Verne Trophy round-the-world record attempt.

After a stormy and unpleasant crossing of the Bay of Biscay – with no sails up, the 110ft catamaran was still blown along at up to 20 knots – MacArthur has hooked into the northeast trade winds.

"Today we will be downwind sailing and are in the trade winds heading for the equator," she reported by satellite phone. "We're smoking, doing 26 knots of boat speed right now…making good miles south."

The first few days at sea took their toll of both boat and crew members. K2 left Plymouth into the teeth of big north Atlantic storm, but MacArthur was afraid of missing the "launch" from directionally favourable northerly winds.

"It has been difficult for a few of the crew since the start — very rough conditions, everybody was tired, and starting in 60 knots was hard," she said. "But in some ways it was a good way to kick off, as everybody was thinking of the safety of themselves and the boat. The boat is going really well and the sails are in good condition."

MacArthur and her 13 crew members must continually watch the clock and pace themselves against the record set by the French skipper and crew of Orange last July. Yesterday, after two days at sea, she calculated that they were about six hours behind.

However, in the light of the far-from-ideal departure conditions, nobody on board K2 considered that too significant. Perhaps more worrying is the stunning performance of the trimaran Geronimo.

The French multihull, skippered by Olivier de Kersauson, left France three weeks ago on a Jules Verne record attempt and is already well into the Southern Ocean, south of the Crozet Archipelago and en route to Cape Horn.

De Kersauson, who broke the record for the first time in 1997 on board Sport Elec, has not put a foot wrong since crossing the start line and is reckoned to be slightly more than two days ahead of the pace set by Orange.

While MacArthur is confident that with average luck from the weather gods her team can trim the 64-day record, a sub 60-day target set by this new breed of mutlihull would be a big task for her team.

The promised webcam access via the internet has been affected by storm damage. Communications equipment has taken a hammering from violent waves, limiting the internet systems to lower-speed connections. This will have an impact on the weather information that they can receive on board, and the video content they can send back.

From *The Sunday Times*, 2nd February 2003

1   How does Keith Wheatley bring out Ellen MacArthur's skill and bravery?

2   What do the quotations from MacArthur contribute to the report?

3   Select the facts that are used in John Wragg's article about Paula Radcliffe and comment on the way they are used.

4   What reasons does Gebrselassie give for admiring Paula Radcliffe?

5   What can you deduce about Gebrselassie's attitudes and biases from what he says about Paula Radcliffe?

Article 2

All hail my hero Paula says Haile

JOHN WRAGG

EXCLUSIVE

GREATEST: Radcliffe has won the finest compliment of all from the legendary Gebrselassie

HAILE GEBRSELASSIE, the greatest distance runner of all time, has paid Paula Radcliffe the ultimate compliment, saying: "She's my hero. Only the top 20 men marathon runners in the world could beat her."

The Ethiopian said Radcliffe had turned distance running on its head, shocking the previously-dominant African nations who were now having to work harder than ever to catch her up.

"Paula doesn't run like a woman – she runs like a man," said Gebrselassie, who will bid for his third Olympic track gold in Athens next year before switching to marathon running himself.

His admiration for Radcliffe, following her astonishing step up from track to marathon, is immense. "Only the top 20 men in the world could beat her," he said. "I admire her so much. She is my hero.

"When I first saw Paula run many years ago, I watched her style with her bobbing head and asked how she could run so well and be in so much pain. For years, there were only tears for her because Paula would always be beaten. For my country, Ethiopia, we smiled because we were the winners, but I have watched with awe how Paula has not let those years beat her.

"Before the London Marathon last year, I told my countrywomen they would not win, that Paula Radcliffe would win. They looked at me strangely and said it was not possible because it was Paula's first marathon.

"But everyone knows now I was right. The Africans had become so used to winning that they did not think it could happen.

"They were shocked by Paula in London and could not believe the world record she ran in Chicago. Neither could I when I saw her time. "Now Paula leads and the Africans are following. It is something they have never had to cope with from a European. Believe me, they are all still shocked."

Gebrselassie sees in Radcliffe an echo of himself in the daunting amount of work she puts into training.

"When I learnt how hard she trained, I knew one day she would be the best," he said. "When you train hard, up and down the big hills, you might not like it, but it makes it easy when it comes to the races.

"My body is getting older and I have to realise that and change a little, but I still work very, very hard in Ethiopia. I do not miss any days because I know I will need that training when it comes to my races in Europe. Paula is the same in her attitude.

"She is not afraid of the pain of working hard."

Radcliffe is considering running the Olympic marathon, but Gebrselassie is already discounting the men's race, saying Athens will be too hot and the conditions too tough. He opens his season indoors in Birmingham on February 21 by trying to break the two-mile record at the Norwich Union grand prix.

It would be the 17th record of an astonishing career which has brought him two 10,000m Olympic golds and seven world championships.

There is another world championship for him to go for in the summer in Paris, then the Olympic 10,000m hat-trick a year later and onwards to the marathon…trying to follow his hero's example.

From the *Daily Express*, 5th February 2003

6   Compare the two articles in terms of:
  ◆ their purposes
  ◆ the ways they praise their subjects
  ◆ the presentational devices used.

7   How does the language used in Article 1 differ from that used in Article 2? Select some examples from each article. What do you think the effect of the language is?

Introduction

In Paper 2 of the English examination, you will be answering a question on poems from different cultures and traditions (grouped as Clusters 1 and 2 in your AQA *Anthology*). Your answer will be worth up to 15 % of your total marks in English. This chapter will explain how you can prepare yourself well for the exam and also give you some pointers as to what you ought to be thinking about at this stage.

By now, you should have been through the poems several times in class. You should also have been reading them on your own. Many students think that reading the poems in class is enough. It isn't. Everyone who reads a poem is an individual and so everyone will have a slightly different response. Your response can only be developed well for the exam if you've read the poems many times *for yourself*, so that you know them thoroughly.

The exam question will ask you to refer to at least two poems. You need to have lots of practice comparing parts of poems, so that you can then go on to make links between them with confidence.

Tip! *Read and compare two poems you have studied, every day, for two weeks.*

Assessment Objectives and how to meet them

As you reread these poems, you will need to think about the sorts of things the examiner is going to ask you. To do this, you need to understand the Assessment Objectives that you will be tested on. The examiner who marks your paper will be looking at how closely you fulfil these Assessment Objectives:

- ❏ Read, with insight and engagement, making appropriate references to texts and developing and sustaining interpretations of them.

- ❏ Select material appropriate to purpose, collate material from different sources, and make cross references.

- ❏ Understand and evaluate how writers use linguistic, structural and presentational devices to achieve their effects, and comment on ways language varies and changes.

Look at the individual Assessment Objectives in the panels, below.
The bulleted points explain what you need to do to meet these objectives.

Read with insight and engagement, making appropriate references to texts and developing and sustaining interpretations of them.

Read with insight and engagement
- Think about things from the point of view of the poet and perhaps of the people who are portrayed in the poems. These may not always be the same.
- Understand what the words imply and suggest, as well as what they tell you directly.

Make appropriate references to texts
- Show you understand what the poems are about and what the poet is saying.
- Identify and describe the ideas, feelings and attitudes in the poems.

Develop and sustain interpretations of them
- Be so familiar with the poems that you become interested yourself in what they have to say and how they say it, developing your own ideas about them.
- Think about different ways in which the poems or parts of the poems can be interpreted. Not everyone will connect so easily, for example, with the issues about having a second language and being worried about losing the first one (see *from* 'Search for My Tongue' by Sujata Bhatt); however, we can all identify with the idea of our 'tongue' – our ways of expressing ourself – being inadequate.

Select material appropriate to purpose, collate material from different sources, and make cross references.

Select material appropriate to purpose and collate material from different sources
- Plan your answer carefully so that everything you write is directly relevant to the question you are asked. This is an important examination skill.

Make cross references
- Link the two poems by comparing them.

Understand and evaluate how writers use linguistic, structural and presentational devices to achieve their effects, and comment on ways language varies and changes.

Linguistic
- Understand what devices of language the poets use and what the effect of these is.
- Explain why you think the poet uses the language he or she does and whether this changes during the course of the poem (and if so, why).
- Explain how the language used in one poem is different from the language used in the poem you are comparing it with. Decide why you think this is and explain what effect it has on you, the reader.

Structural
- Have several things to say about the structure of each poem, by thinking about the ways the beginning, middle and end relate to each other. Also think about why the poet has decided to break the poem up into verses (stanzas) or not.

Presentational
- Have other things to say about the effects you think are achieved by the poet's choices of layout, punctuation, the arrangement on the page and the use of capital letters.

Evaluate
- Comment on what you think is particularly effective and telling about a poem and what makes you think this.

Cultures and traditions

The National Curriculum (the programme of study that all schools follow) says that students should study texts from different cultures and traditions. Think about what 'different cultures and traditions' means and then consider how the poems you are studying link with this idea.

Some poets write about their own culture.

Some poets write about two cultures, having moved from one to another.

Some poets write about two different cultures within one particular country.

CULTURE =
people's ideas, attitudes, values and beliefs

TRADITION =
a set pattern of behaviour, passed down through the generations

Some poets look at traditions that they feel are valuable.

Some poets look at traditions that they feel are restrictive, or out of date.

Some poets look at traditions that contrast with what they now believe in, or are accustomed to.

 Remember! *The poet may or may not be writing about his or her own culture. The characters in the poems may or may not voice the poet's own ideas.*

Checklist ✅

While you are revising the poems, use this checklist to consider how they link to the concept of different cultures and traditions:

- ✔ Where does each poet come from and which place is he or she writing about?
- ✔ What is the poet's attitude to the cultures and traditions featured in his or her poems?
- ✔ Contrast the cultures and traditions in the poems with the cultures and traditions you were brought up with and are familiar with. This will help you to evaluate the importance, significance and influence of culture and tradition on the ways people behave, think and feel.

Of course, not *all* exam questions will ask you about *all* of these things, but it is nevertheless useful for you to concentrate on them during revision. This way, you will be really confident about any question that might come up.

Comparing poems

Every question in the exam will ask you to compare one poem with a second poem. You need to practise making precise links between the poems in order to bring out their distinctiveness and to be able to make clear, sharp points of comparison.

Think about the following question, then choose two poems. Fill out the chart below to help make your thoughts clear.

Question

Compare the ways in which two poets present what they have to say in their poems.

Write about:
- what they have to say
- the methods they use to say it
- what cultures and traditions they draw on and write about
- how effectively you think they convey what they have to say.

Note

This question is probably more general than the one you are going to be asked in the exam, but it is a useful one for revision.

Area	Poem 1	Poem 2
Ideas		
Feelings		
Attitudes		
Language (and effects)		
Structure (and effects)		
Other aspects of presentation (and effects)		
Cultures		
Traditions		
Your evaluation		

Now think about how you could turn this information into an essay. You have already got the skeleton of a plan, which allows you to take each area in turn and make comparisons and draw contrasts between the poems.

Follow this thought process to help you make notes before you start writing your essay:

1 What are the precise points of comparison and contrast between the two poems?

2 Think of topic sentences with which to begin each paragraph: how will you make a clear distinction between the poems as you tackle each area?

3 How are you going to link your ideas most effectively?

4 What is your opening sentence going to be? It needs to make the examiner/reader interested in what you have to say.

5 What (for you) really clinches the similarity or difference between the poems?

In the exam, you only have 45 minutes to make a plan and write your essay. If you want to practise writing an essay based on the above, allow yourself an hour, as this particular question covers more than an exam question will.

 Take a few minutes to plan your answer before you start writing. This will ensure that you don't run out of time or forget anything.

P.E.C. technique

A very useful technique to remember in your exam is:

Point ➤ Example (quotation or close reference to detail from the poem) ➤ Comment

If you use this technique, then the examiner will be able to see what you have to say about the poem, what details you are basing your ideas on and why you think it matters.

Tom Leonard involves the reader directly in the poem (point) by refering to him/her in his Glaswegian dialect as 'wanna yoo / scruff' (example), but this is much more challenging then John Agard's polite request (comment) for the reader to 'Excuse me' (example) at the beginning of his poem.

How your work will be marked

It's helpful in revision to remind yourself of the way the mark scheme works so that you can try to achieve as high marks as possible. Of course, what you write will depend on the question asked and it's vital to make sure that every sentence you write is directly relevant to the task set. However, the way you write will probably be very similar whatever the question.

Grade Descriptors

In the grid below are the Grade Descriptors. These describe the skills that you need to demonstrate to reach each grade. The examiner will be judging your work, using these Grade Descriptors, whichever exam question you answer. Look carefully at these Descriptors. Can you identify the way you usually write and see what you need to improve on to reach the next grade?

Grade	Description of skills
Grade U	◆ some awareness of one or more texts
Grade G	◆ simple comment ◆ begins to support simple comment ◆ awareness of some aspects of presentation
Grade F	◆ begins to support simple comment ◆ reference to appropriate detail ◆ statement of some aspects of presentation
Grade E	◆ extended comment ◆ generalization on the text as a whole ◆ appropriate reference and some use of quotation ◆ simple comment on some aspects of presentation ◆ some awareness of a writer at work
Grade D	◆ awareness of feelings, attitudes, ideas ◆ range of comment supported by textual detail ◆ comment on effects achieved by writer
Grade C	◆ understanding of feelings, attitudes, ideas ◆ effective use of textual detail ◆ some cross reference ◆ awareness of authorial techniques and purpose
Grade B	◆ appreciation of feelings, attitudes and ideas ◆ effective use of textual detail ◆ integrated cross reference ◆ understanding of a variety of writers' techniques
Grade A	◆ exploration of and empathy with writers' ideas and attitudes ◆ references integrated with argument ◆ analysis of variety of writers' techniques
Grade A*	◆ consistent insight and convincing/imaginative interpretation ◆ conceptualized response ◆ close textual analysis ◆ rigorous comparison

Of course, you will see that a lot of these descriptions, particularly for the higher grades, are about the range of material you use as well as the depth of the comment you make. It's not possible, therefore, to see from extracts what grade the whole essay will get. However, you can see from the extracts below some of the methods of writing which are characteristic of certain levels of achievement.

Students' answers

Answer 1

Examiner's comments:
- there is a simple comment
- the candidate states own response
- no reference to detail
- no awareness of presentation
- Grade G.

> Agard uses different methods to describe and to educate you in al the different cultures in 'Half-Caste'. He uses language which means you are not a full man, not totally disabled not nearly disabled and nearly a full man but he is missing something which is needed to make you a full man or woman which makes him feel Half-Caste.
>
> It is like being not white but not black either so you are called half-caste which is very wrong to say about someone just because they are not the normal.
>
> The poem which has the most influence on me is the Half-caste poem because it makes the man that is involved in the poem sound like he is going to have no life in front of him.

Answer 2

Examiner's comments:
- several simple comments
- reference to some appropriate detail
- statements on some aspects of presentation (foreign language, letters missing)
- comments not really supported by detail
- Grade F.

> 'Search for my Tongue' is about a person who forgets their native tongue. This means that the person was from somewhere, but moved to England and she thinks that she had forgotten the language of where she came from.
>
> I like how this poem is set out because of how, in the first paragraph she is taking about how she has forgot to speak her own language, but as she goes to sleep her dreams are spoken in that language. And you can see her language written down on the page.
>
> John Agard talks of other things which some people find pretty but which he himself sees as half-cast. He talks about the weather, Picasso and Tchaikovsky. He describes himself as half a man and he also writes that way. You can see it on the page because he writes with letters missing out of words all the time.

Answer 3

Examiner's comments:
- beginnings of extended comment
- a little appropriate reference to detail
- simple comment on one aspect of presentation (tries to show the effect of the introduction of the Gujerati)
- Grade E.

'Search for my Tongue' is laid out very normal to start off with and at about line 17 the lines are written in Gujerati then goes back to English. This is done to build an image in our heads. We start to read the poem then stop when she says 'but overnight when I dream'. This means that in her dream her mother tongue grows back. Sujata Bhatt has set up her poem to make sure you read, stop, think, then realise that the Gujerati written is only in her dream. The poem is like a mission poem where somebody is searching for something.

Answer 4

Examiner's comments:
- aware of ideas and feelings
- extended supported comment
- comment on effect achieved by writer (in the last two sentences)
- Grade D.

In 'Hurricane Hits England' the woman in the poem misses her home country and it makes her feel at home when a hurricane hits England because it reminds her of home and it brings her closer to home. Everyone is scared and wants to run away but she is on the hurricane's side and is glad it has come. At the end she realizes that 'home is where the heart is' and when the poem says 'the earth is the earth is the earth' it means that the earth is the same wherever you are and that we have no control. This is when the realization sets in. When she writes 'even as you short-circuit us' Grace Nichols makes you stop at the end of 'short' because you have to go on to the next line. Also you are 'cut off' from the sentence just as the electricity is 'cut off'.

Answer 5

Examiner's comments:
- understanding of ideas and attitudes
- some use of cross reference
- awareness of authorial purpose
- implicit reference to technique ('builds up to his anger')
- better on meanings than techniques
- Grade C.

'Nothing's Changed' is a piece of protest which represents the different life-styles - one being black, a lifestyle of poverty, and the other white, a lifestyle of luxury, at this time. The poem describes the culture to be very segregated. He starts off giving a description of 'district six' and builds up to his anger of how the white people dominate the black and coloured people.

He uses emphasis on the two life styles.

Line 38 states 'wipe your fingers on your jeans' which is much different to the 'up-market haute cuisine' where the white people eat. Tatamkulu Afrika shows that there is no connection between these two groups of people. Line 23 'guard at the gatepost.' This signifies no black people or those who are not white are to be permitted to eat in this restaurant. The black people know where they belong and where they will be accepted.

Similar to 'Nothing's Changed' 'Presents from my Aunts in Pakistan' also represents two types of lifestyle but it doesn't show one culture being oppressed by another. It shows how often one culture wants what the other has.

Answer 6

Examiner's comments:
- understanding of ideas and feelings
- effective use of textual detail
- understanding of the writer's techniques (in 'Blessing')
- clear explanation of own response
- effective cross reference
- the answer as a whole (this is an extract) dealt with a range of the writers' techniques
- Grade B.

In 'Blessing' the poet uses various methods to show just how important and how much joy water brings to the asian community. 'The skin cracks like a pod'. This is an effective simile as it outlines the dryness of parched skin, comparing this to the brittleness of a ripe seed pod - outlining the basic need for water.

The poem goes on to say 'There is never enough' which is a clever way that the poet has used to evoke our emotions, because we indeed do have enough of it, but some asian communities don't as they struggle in their environment.

'Blessing' examines what people have never had enough of, whereas 'Island Man' looks at how a man who moved from a Caribbean island to London is constantly reminded of what he has left behind.

Both poems have a strong influence on me but 'Blessing' dominates my emotions the most as it makes me feel slightly guilty that I don't appreciate the sheer gift of water and always seem to focus on the importance of materialistic things to make me happy, like clothes, shoes and jewellery.

Answer 7

Examiner's comments:
- explores the ideas and feelings in 'Nothing's Changed'
- empathy with writer's ideals and attitudes
- reference integrated with argument
- analysis of two techniques
- telling and illuminating cross reference
- essay as a whole analyses several techniques
- Grade A.

On returning to District Six Afrika feels angry and frustrated as 'nothing's changed'. Apartheid still exists, and Afrika writes that 'no sign says it is, but we know where we belong'. The connection is so strong, but still his 'hands burn for a bomb, to shiver down the glass'.

He wants to blow the place up. He wants to remove the separation which exists. Therefore, for Afrika, District Six has immense power, in that it is able to trigger emotions as violent as wanting to bomb the place, shown in the dramatic image and the powerful alliteration of 'burn' and 'bomb'.

There is also a strong connection between people and the place in which they live in 'Presents from my Aunts in Pakistan'. Moniza Alvi was born in Pakistan but moved to England when she was young. As a result she is unsure as to her identity. In her birthplace, Pakistan, her Aunts send her exotic sensuous clothes to remind her of who she really is, and it disturbs her. Ironically they would prefer to have clothes from Marks and Spencer to the clothes they have sent her.

Answer 8

Examiner's comments:
- ◆ consistent insight
- ◆ some imaginative interpretation
- ◆ conceptualized comparison
- ◆ some close textual analysis
- ◆ Grade A*.

Alvi explores the idea of an Indian girl exploring her motherland through simple presents sent by her aunts. Though she had never really seen Pakistan, she is still somehow connected to it and simultaneously has the desire to adapt to her current land and the desire to get to know her motherland. The poem thus explores the way moving country can create the confusion of 'no fixed nationality'. Meanwhile Grace Nichols presents the image of a man isolated by the dreary 'dull North Circular roar' who can only dream of the sights and sounds of his homeland where there were real 'sands' and 'blue surf', the 'emerald' of the island and the 'wild seabirds' contrasting with the 'grey metallic' look of London's cars.

'Presents from my Aunts in Pakistan' explores the connection between places and people with the very interesting device of the presents. Through the poem metaphorical analysis is done with a neutral ambiguous tone, inviting the reader to participate in the girl's dilemma. The very exoticness of the objects and the theme of self-discovery creates empathy with the reader, with the personal self obsessed perspective of the poem creating intimacy.

Introduction

You have two pieces of writing to do in the English examination, one in the second half of Paper 1 and one in the second half of Paper 2.

Assessment Objectives and how to meet them

To gain the highest marks that you can for your writing, you need to understand what the examiner is looking for. He or she will be judging how well you meet the Assessment Objectives for writing, which are listed below.

> ❏ Communicate clearly and imaginatively, using and adapting forms for different readers and purposes.
>
> ❏ Organize ideas into sentences, paragraphs and whole texts using a variety of structural and linguistic features.
>
> ❏ Use a range of sentence structures effectively with accurate punctuation and spelling.

Now look at the individual Assessment Objectives in the panels below. The bulleted points explain what you need to do to meet these objectives.

Communicate clearly and imaginatively, using and adapting forms for different readers and purposes.

Communicate clearly and imaginatively
- Think and plan carefully before you begin to write.
- Use your imagination to make sure that what you write is as interesting as it can be.

Use and adapt forms for different readers and purposes
- Make sure you write in the form you are asked to write in (e.g. a letter, an article).
- Be clear about whom you are writing for if it tells you in the question (e.g. a headteacher, governors, a friend, adults, readers of a local newspaper).
- Make sure you concentrate on the purpose of the writing. This will be in bold letters in the question (e.g. argue, persuade, advise, inform, explain, describe).

Organize ideas into sentences, paragraphs and whole texts using a variety of structural and linguistic features.

Sentences
- Make sure you write in sentences but vary their construction and length.

Paragraphs
- Paragraph properly, making suitable links between the paragraphs where you can, in order to allow the reader to follow what you have to say.

Structural features
- Structure your writing carefully. This can only be done if you have made a plan first.

Linguistic features
- Vary the language you use and make sure that it is appropriate for the purpose of the writing and for the audience.

> **Use a range of sentence structures effectively with accurate punctuation and spelling.**
>
> **Sentence structure**
> ◆ Make sure you use simple, compound and complex sentences, with full stops in the right places.
>
> **Accurate punctuation and spelling**
> ◆ Use clear, accurate punctuation and an appropriate range in order to make your meaning clear and your work easy to read (e.g. commas, full stops, exclamation marks, question marks, inverted commas for speech, underlining for book titles, even semi-colons and colons, if you know how to use them properly).
> ◆ Make your spelling as accurate and consistent as possible.

Planning and checking

You have 45 minutes for each piece of writing but you are not expected to write for more than 35 minutes. Five minutes are set aside for planning your work and five minutes for checking.

Planning

This is an important aspect of all parts of the examination but one which is often skimped or neglected. Your teachers will have told you how important planning is, but very few people do plan properly when it comes to the examination itself and this often leads them to gain lower marks than they would have done had they spent their time properly.

Allow five minutes to plan your work. There are many different ways to plan and you should, by now, have worked out which works best for you.

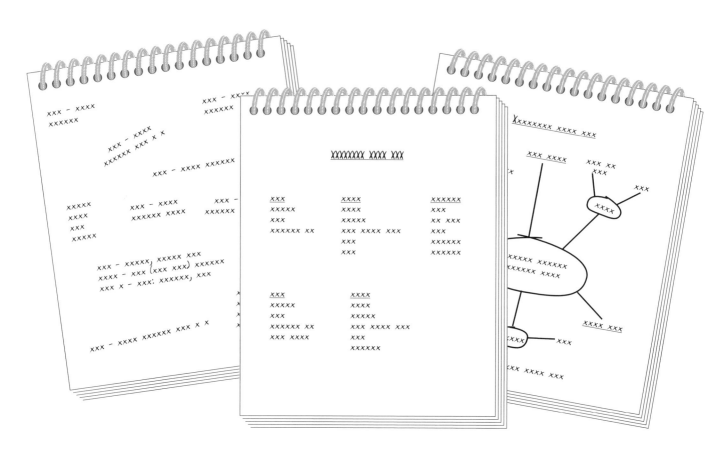

Tip! *Don't write a plan in sentences. Just jot down the different aspects of the topic that you are going to cover. Some people like to list aspects of the style they are going to use as well as the main points they are going to make.*

It doesn't matter which kind of plan you use, but whichever you choose, make sure that you sequence your points after you have brainstormed or scattered or listed them. Sequencing will enable you to organize your answer well, so the examiner can read your piece easily and doesn't have to keep stopping to think about what you've just said and where you are going next. Order your points so that you can make links between them.

Checking

You should spend five minutes checking your work. This can make a big difference to the marks you get. It's often hard to be critical of what you have written immediately after you have written it, but here are some basic things that you should ask yourself:

Is my spelling accurate?

Have I used a comma where I should have used a full stop?

Are all my full stops in the right places?

Are the paragraphs in a logical order?

Have I used a variety of punctuation accurately?

Is my spelling as consistent as I can make it?

Have I used paragraphs? If not, I can put paragraph marks in where I want them.

Even the students who are going to get the highest marks can make good use of this five minutes checking time. When you have asked yourself the questions above, there are other things that you can check.

- ✔ The opening is as interesting as you can make it.
- ✔ The last sentence clinches what you have written and leaves the reader interested.
- ✔ You have used a variety of appropriate punctuation.
- ✔ You haven't repeated words too often.
- ✔ You have used words which are interesting and accurate.

Examiners don't mind you crossing things out as long as they can read what you want them to mark. Of course, it's best to think first before you write, but the examiners want to see the best that you can do, and this rarely happens without you making some alterations and corrections.

Different kinds of writing

You have a choice of writing tasks on each of the two papers. There will probably be four questions in each writing section.

> Paper 1 tests writing to ARGUE, PERSUADE, ADVISE.
>
> Paper 2 tests writing to INFORM, EXPLAIN, DESCRIBE.

There will always be one question on each of the three words (in the 'triplets') and then one, or possibly more, which mixes the three words.

Which question you choose to answer is important because you may feel more comfortable with one type of writing than another. Sometimes you might like the topic best in one question but the type of writing in another. You need to decide which question will allow you to show off your strengths best.

Whichever type of writing you choose, you should use some of the key words and phrases (known as 'discourse' features) normally associated with that type of writing. Some of these discourse features will be used in more than one kind of writing.

Look at the following panels which focus on different types of writing. Read the words and phrases often associated with the different types of writing. Look also at some of the stylistic features associated with each type of writing.

Paper 1

Argue

The most important aspect...
Sometimes...
On the other hand...
Firstly...
Secondly...
Thirdly...
However...
Nevertheless...
On balance...

Moreover...
Despite the view that...
Nothwithstanding...
Research shows that...
The evidence clearly shows that...
Another factor to be considered is...
Opponents declare...but...

Some other features:

◆ formal language
◆ balanced sentences
◆ people's opinions (real or made up)
◆ specific examples of situations
◆ range and variety of points
◆ countering opposing points of view
◆ a neat conclusion.

Persuade

Some people think...
It would be useful to consider...
Do they really think that...
In my experience...
What would the consequences be...
Common sense dictates that...
What would happen if...
All reasonable people think...

By far the best solution would be...
Do we really want to...
It is frightening to think that...
We need to make sure that...
I have no doubt at all that...
Imagine what would happen if...
I am sure you will agree that...
There can be only one conclusion...

Some other features:

◆ emotive language
◆ apparent balance
◆ mixture of first, second and third person
◆ some short sentences
◆ identify with audience by using 'we'
◆ perhaps some attempt to shock reader into agreement
◆ varied choice of adverbs and adjectives
◆ some 'literary' devices such as alliteration, groups of three.

Advise

You might be able to...	One solution might be to...
Think about...	Another possibility would be to...
Make sure that you...	If you don't...then you could...
You should be careful to...	Be careful to...
Don't...	In order to avoid...
If you...then you could...	I think you should...
I understand that you feel...	Be confident about...
Don't worry if...	If , on the other hand, then...

Some other features:
- formal language
- close relationship with audience
- providing reasons for a course of action
- empathy with the audience's problem
- several suggestions about what to do
- use of modal verbs (e.g. might, could, should)
- build the confidence of the reader
- address the reader directly in the second person (you)
- use imperatives (e.g. 'you should', 'make sure that you', 'be careful to')
- raise questions and give answers
- perhaps sometimes use bullet points for lists
- lead to a clear conclusion about action to be taken.

Paper 2

Inform

There are many kinds of...	If you want to...then you need to...
The one I am most interested in is...	In order to begin you need to...
The pleasure I find in...	Make sure that you...
The excitement lies in...	Some people enjoy...
By far the most interesting aspect...	Other kinds of...

Some other features:
- clear introduction
- provide a context for what you are going to write
- wide range of different aspects of the topic
- detail
- technical language, perhaps explained briefly
- systematic and logical organization
- use of personal experience
- use of present tense
- clear links between paragraphs
- unusual and interesting detail specific to the subject.

Explain

Because...	The first thing to do is...
Another reason...	Later on I...
Although...	Ultimately...
Nevertheless...	Contrary to popular belief...
The most important...	As a result...
Above all else...	Consequently...
Despite the fact that...	Inevitably...

Some other features:
- range of reasons
- range of appropriate detail
- specific examples of different kinds to support explanation
- range of responses to 'why'
- range of responses to 'how'
- different points expanded and linked.

Describe

It is more difficult to pick out particular words and phrases which might be useful here but there are a range of features characteristic of effective descriptive writing which you could draw on:

- wide range of appropriate detail
- use of modifiers such as adjectives and adverbs
- use of colour
- use of senses: sight, touch – perhaps texture, hearing, taste, sound
- words to convey feelings and atmosphere
- use of metaphor and simile, perhaps use of personification
- denser language than in many of the other forms
- perhaps personal reactions
- variation of sentence length and type
- rich, varied, perhaps unusual vocabulary.

Purpose, audience and form

As well as mentioning one or more types of writing, the exam question may also tell you about the *purpose, audience* and *form* of your writing. In Paper 1 particularly you may be asked to write one of the following:

> ➤ a letter
> ➤ an article
> ➤ an advice sheet
> ➤ a letter to an editor
> ➤ a report
> ➤ a speech
> ➤ a piece with no clear form or audience.

Letter

You need to be clear whether this is a formal or an informal letter. If it is a formal letter you need to include:

◆ your own address at the top right hand corner
◆ the address of the person it is going to underneath against the left hand margin
◆ the date
◆ a formal greeting (e.g. 'Dear Sir', 'Dear Madam', 'Dear Mr Jones')
◆ a formal sign-off ('Yours faithfully' if you don't know the person; 'Yours sincerely' if you do know the person)
◆ your signature
◆ perhaps your name written clearly underneath (if your signature is a squiggle).

If it is an informal letter you just need:
◆ your own address in the top right-hand corner
◆ the date
◆ an informal greeting (e.g. 'Dear Gran', 'Dear John')
◆ an informal sign-off (e.g. 'Love')
◆ your signature.

Be careful to match your language to the person the letter is going to. If it is to someone with status or to someone you don't know, then you must use formal speech. Make sure you don't offend them; for instance, you will be unlikely to persuade them if you are insulting or use bullying tactics.

Think carefully about what they might know or not know; don't use language or slang that they may not understand. If it is an informal letter then you would expect to take certain things for granted; don't explain who people you both know are. In an informal letter you can use chatty language, but the sort of chatty language might depend on whether you are writing to your Granny or writing to your best mate.

Tip!

Whichever kind of letter it is, make sure that what you write is relevant to the topic. If you are writing to someone you know well, for example, keep the main letter about the topic, but add anything of a personal nature in a PS at the end.

Article

You might well be asked to write an article for a newspaper. Think carefully about the sort of newspaper you are writing for (i.e. tabloid or broadsheet) and adapt your language accordingly. An article for *The Sun*, for example, would be very different in language from an article for *The Times*.

You are being asked to write the text for the newspaper. You don't have to set it out in columns but you do need to use those features of writing which you might expect in a newspaper. These will be:

- a headline
- maybe a banner headline
- maybe some sub-headings
- maybe a strapline
- the kinds of paragraphs used (short for tabloids or longer for broadsheets)
- the sort of formal and/or informal language usually used by the newspaper that you are writing for.

Tip! *You don't need to bother about pictures or cartoons or layout. Concentrate on the quality and accuracy of your writing.*

Advice sheet

These take many forms so there are no hard and fast rules. However, you may need to use lists in your writing so it is useful to think about how easily and swiftly these might be read by the reader. You might want to use:

- underlined headings
- a title
- bullet points.

Organization is key. Make sure that you group the different kinds of advice carefully into paragraphs or sections. You need to take the reader through the topic in a logical order so that the advice is coherent and clear.

Letter to an editor

Tip! *You have to be careful with this form because there is really a dual audience: the editor and the readers of the newspaper.*

You need to write it as a formal letter, as it is going to someone of status and to someone you don't know. 'Dear Editor' is the best greeting and 'Yours faithfully' with your signature is the best sign-off. Note that sometimes editors don't include the address of the person writing but use the paper's standard format for printing such letters.

Your writing needs to be close to the style of the newspaper because it is the newspaper readers who are the 'real' audience for your letter. You can, of course, use some informal features, depending on the purpose of the letter. It is likely that you will be expressing your own argument, or trying to persuade the readers of something. In this case you want to use the common features of argue and persuade writing.

Report

Reports are usually a formal type of writing. They are mainly factual or writing which groups opinion for some purpose. They need to be clearly organized and usually have:

◆ a headline
◆ sub-headings
◆ an introduction
◆ a body of evidence or discussion
◆ a conclusion.

Speech

Tip!

You need to be careful here because although you are asked for a speech it is actually a written speech and so it needs to obey the rules of writing even though its purpose is to be delivered orally.

Make sure that you write your speech obeying the rules of writing, using:

◆ appropriate punctuation
◆ sentences
◆ paragraphs
◆ technical written accuracy.

Many of the structures you use will be those of speech but they will have to be recorded as if they are writing.

Remember!

1 *You are likely to be much more rhetorical in your speech than in many other forms of writing.*

2 *You need to keep the listeners' interest throughout so make sure that you include all the normal signals of speech to do that: rhetorical questions; repetition; mixture of simple, compound and complex sentences and non-sentences (i.e. those without a main verb); dramatic devices to keep the listeners' interest.*

3 *Draw on all your Speaking and Listening experiences during the course to think about how to make your speech appropriate to its audience.*

As well as this, you have to think about the same things as in all the other forms of writing. You need to make sure that your register and vocabulary are suitable for the audience you are addressing and that the structure of your speech is very clear and can be easily grasped by a listener.

No obvious form or audience

Sometimes a task doesn't stipulate the form or the audience. You might be asked to explain something, for example, but the question doesn't tell you about a specific form to write in or a specific person to address your writing to. This often happens on Paper 2. When this happens:

◆ write as yourself – you as an examination candidate
◆ write for the examiner reader who is an English teacher
◆ write to show off your writing skills.

In the examination

So far, I have been trying to help you to revise systematically for the examination by looking at what you are expected to do and by covering some of the things that you are meant to know and have studied. In this next section, I want to look specifically at *how* these things can be put into action in the examination room by taking some examples.

Before you choose which question to answer, you need to be confident about what the question is asking you to do. Look for the key words of the task and use these as the basis for your planning. I will cover a few examples for you and then give you some other examples to practise on.

Writing to argue or persuade

Imagine you are faced with this question:

Question

It has recently been suggested that government ministers are thinking about making education compulsory until the age of eighteen.

Write a letter to your MP. Argue why he or she should or should not support this idea and persuade him of your own point of view.

Remember to:
- write a letter
- use language suitable for an MP to read
- argue
- persuade the MP.

Now follow these steps:

1   First, identify the key words of the task and then remember what characteristics of writing you need to use.

2   Think about the best way of presenting your ideas:
   - argue writing
   - use words of argument
   - argue for OR against
   - use language suitable to be read by an MP
   - make a list of your arguments
   - then use persuasive techniques
   - think about what sorts of arguments an MP might be persuaded by
   - use language appropriate to be read by an MP
   - form of a letter
   - formal letter – two addresses and Dear Sir (or use the name)
   - ends 'Yours faithfully'.

3   Now plan your content. List your arguments for or against.

4   Decide on the order of your arguments. Perhaps lead up to your strongest point. You might choose to present the arguments first and then the persuasion, or you might decide that you want to try to persuade him or her about each argument in turn. In any case the sequencing of your material will be important in creating your desired impact.

Writing to describe

Here is a task that does not specify a particular purpose or audience:

Question

Describe the room you are sitting in.

Now follow these steps:

1   Briefly jot down ideas for your material:
   ◆ task is to describe a room
   ◆ variety of detail: objects, furniture, any people, what is unusual
   ◆ perhaps what room shows about owner or inhabitants
   ◆ atmosphere, mood, colours
   ◆ what fits in and what doesn't
   ◆ senses: sight, texture, sounds heard, smells, tastes
   ◆ comparisons: similes and metaphors
   ◆ use of imagery, alliteration, personification.

2   Now think about how to sequence the material and make links between the different paragraphs. Can you build the description up towards some sort of climax? Might it be a good idea to come back at the end to the way the piece started?

3   When you are actually writing, think about:
   ◆ using adjectives where appropriate
   ◆ using adverbs sometimes
   ◆ finding precise and unusual words
   ◆ interesting the reader by variation of vocabulary and sentence structure
   ◆ whether you can create any surprises for the reader by withholding some information
   ◆ ending in a strong and striking way.

Practice questions

Practise the process of thinking about the task, then making plans by working on the following:

1   *Write an article for a broadsheet newspaper in which you **argue** the case for more money being spent on up-to-date equipment for schools.*

   Remember to:
   ● *write an article*
   ● *write the text for a broadsheet newspaper*
   ● *use language appropriate for an argument.*

2   *You have undertaken some research among pupils in your school about the length and organization of the school day. Write a report for the Chair of Governors in which you* **persuade** *him or her that particular changes should be made.*

Remember to:
- *write a report*
- *use language appropriate for the Chair of Governors to read*
- *use language to persuade.*

3   *Write a report to the manager of your school's catering service* **advising** *him or her of the need to provide a different range of food during the course of the school day.*

Remember to:
- *write a report*
- *use language appropriate for the catering manager to read*
- *use language to advise.*

4   *Choose something you are particularly interested in. Write in such a way as to* **inform** *someone who knows very little about this topic what it consists of and what makes it interesting.*

Remember to:
- *write to inform*
- *inform about the interest*
- *inform about what makes it interesting.*

5   *Your aunt has two children, a boy and a girl, who are about to become teenagers. She has asked you to* **explain** *to her, based on your own experience of being a teenager, what she should look out for as her children grow up, what you think are the main challenges of being and bringing up a teenager and what she should do about likely situations that might arise. Write a letter to her* **explaining** *these things and what you think she should do about typical situations that might arise.*

Remember to:
- *write a letter*
- *use language suitable to explain.*

6   **Describe** *someone you admire. Make sure that you include in your description something about:*
- *what he / she looks like*
- *how he / she dresses*
- *his / her behaviour*
- *his / her interests*
- *his / her responses to other people.*

Different sorts of questions

As you work towards the end of your revision, think about the differences between the kinds of writing you can choose between. Remember many different sorts of questions can be asked about one topic. You have to decide the type of writing that is needed in the answer. For example, all the questions below are about the same topic, but each question requires you to write a different sort of answer. Think about how the answers will differ.

(a) *There are competitions every year for Sportsperson of the Year. Write the script for a radio programme where you* **argue** *the case for your choice to be made Sportsperson of the Year.*

(b) *Imagine that you are a television presenter. Write the script for a programme where you* **persuade** *the viewers that your choice of person should be made Sportsperson of the Year.*

(c) *Write an article for a newspaper where you* **inform** *the readers about the achievements of a particular Sportsperson whom you think is worthy to be called the Sportsperson of the Year.*

(d) **Explain** *clearly why you think your choice should be made Sportsperson of the Year.*

Students' answers

It is difficult to explain the grades of particular pieces of writing from extracts because the mark is based on the piece as a whole. However, the following extracts from students' work highlight some important things that you should think about while you are still in the examination room.

Answers 1–4 are written in response to the following task.

Question

Choose a person who has played an important part in your life.
Explain how this person has been important to you.

Answer 1

This is the first longer paragraph of the two the student wrote.

The person who means a lot to me is because she does everything write and never has any dout into what she want but is very honest and doesn't really know who you are but now's and respects that you do like her and she doesn't tell anyone. She is one of the most amazing things ever born and she knows it but doesn't do much about it. She is a very quiet person keeps her self to her self and dosn't really have relationships very often but when she does they mean a lot to her. She is important to me because I think of her as more than a friend but more like a sister because she is always there for me and she is always there to talk to and comfort you when you are down and feeling like you don't want to do anything ever again, She knows everything about me and that is why she means so much to me. If I wanted someone to help me with a problem she would be the one I would phone And she would help sort it out and maby make the problem turn into a good thing which she does quite often.

Examiner's comments:
- several statements about importance
- person strangely never named or identified
- spelling generally correct but always simple words
- mainly compound sentences; too much use of 'and'
- punctuation astray and inconsistent
- paragraphs missing here
- no clear organization or order of statements
- all very general
- unchecked – errors inconsistent
- Grade F.

Answer 2

This is the whole essay.

A person who has played an important part n my life is Basketball star Michel Jorden. He is my favourite basketball player, he has acheived alot while playing basketball by becoming the best in the world with his shooting skills to how high he can jump, he is an insparation. He as made me see that I can go far With my obsesstion at the game. When I was younger I never knew what I wanted to be when I grow up, but now all I think about 24/7 is basketball, and how good am I?, and is there anything I could do to improve and become better, I also ask myself will I ever become as good as Michel Jorden, and have trainers and close names after me, but all I can do is work hard and keep practicing.

I now play for a National League team which is a high level for my age, But soon I am looking to move to America and play for a professonal team, make it big and become a Star just like Michel Jorden. Until then I will just keep trying.

Examiner's comments:
- rather short answer
- some explanation
- two paragraphs but more would have been effective
- some spelling mistakes
- punctuation mistakes
- explanations undeveloped
- more information than explanation
- E grade.

Answer 3

This is the second half of the essay.

> This person teaches me new things everyday, this person is so wise and full knowledge its unbelievable, this person don't get me wrong is not perfect, they have imperfections, but aren't imperfections what make people? I wouldn't swop this person for the world. There are so many people, people would like to have in their lives. For example David Beckham, Britney Spears, Nsync etc. They only see what is portrayed by television it is not based on any type of reality, whereas the person in my life is all real.
>
> If there is something I don't want to hear this person will tell me, do you want to know why? Because they care & love me and if they see me going in the wrong direction, they will steer me back on the right track.
>
> This person is good to me, they do more good than they will ever know, and I love them more than they will ever know. Want to know who this person is... MY DAD!

Examiner's comments:
- engaged with purpose – some parts explain importance
- attempts to provide some variety of content
- some shaping – we don't find out who it is until the end
- much of the writing asserts rather than explains
- it's unchecked
- there are lots of technical errors
- in some places full stops are missing.
- singular and plural agreements are faulty – 'person' is singular but is then referred to as 'they'
- question mark missing in final sentence
- overall this has some promise; careful checking could have brought this into a notional C grade but as it stands it remains in D.

Answer 4

These two paragraphs come from the middle of a much longer essay.

> David Beckham was a hero, then came World Cup '98 in France. The tournament began with Beckham putting in outstanding performances, including a swerving free-kick against Columbia — he was on 'Cloud Nine.' As England faced fierce rivals Argentina in the Second Round, the blonde, floppy-haired midfielder was shown the Red card. As he paced off the pitch the tear in his eye created such sympathy in me. Tragically, we were defeated on a bitter penalty shoot out.
>
> The next day I opened the newspaper to find an onslaught on Beckham. These views of anger and the idea he had let us down soon spread nationwide — he became the most hated man in Britain. I, however, tried to back him up when in conversation with my friends. If Beckham hadn't played at all, we wouldn't have been there in the first place. He was probably the player of the tournament.

Examiner's comments:
- this is accurate, fluent writing
- there are clear explanations and a variety of detail
- points are developed and elaborated
- one place where there is a comma instead of a full stop
- spelling and syntax are accurate
- interests the reader by some colourful modifiers (blonde, floppy-haired)
- there is a clear link between the paragraphs
- some phrases which could have been more stylishly expressed (see if you can find them and think about how they could have been improved)
- good B grade.

The next three answers (5–7) were written in response to this task.

Question

Describe the room you are sitting in.

Answer 5

This is the student's whole answer.

> The room I'm in it's very big we are lots of students we doing an exam at the moment The room carpet it's green and the chairs are green as well he's got three big heaters but at the moment it's too cold, he got two doors who's very big. At the moment it's too dark we using the lights, the room got sixteen lights. we got ninty three chairs. the room it's quiet and pice.

Examiner's comments:
- short and unextended
- relevant to task
- some very simple description (colours, mood mentioned)
- in sentences but not properly punctuated
- full stops and capital letters unmatched
- spelling of simple words mostly accurate
- no paragraphs
- unchecked
- Grade G.

Answer 6

This is the second half of a descriptive piece.

> The room lit up and I was in my white, flower embroidered evening gown. Sitting in my favourite room. It was perfect. I played with the butterflies, it was all that I would see. My dream world, that was my old reality. Nothing else mattered. No memories. Just the simple sound of butterflies, and me.
>
> I was all that I was, all that I had been, all I had known since I was a child.
>
> I didn't want to return to my life of knowing. Back in that room.
>
> Empty room. My life was gone. The room is still there, but different. No butterflies, nothing. There was no ceiling, just pure, perfect space.
>
> No floor, just dust that rose and fell. Like rain. Soft, light painful rain. Making me cry. I had no memories.
>
> The room was in me.
>
> I was empty. I was not scared, and I had no life.
>
> Sitting in me. The empty room.
>
> Butterfly friends that left me and now were faded.
>
> The room faded.

Examiner's comments:
- this is ambitious writing
- has an idea and follows it through
- not much description of the room
- more a meditation upon being in the room
- often rather clipped expression
- paragraphing often seems random; too many short paragraphs
- over-uses the same devices – such as minor sentences
- technically accurate but lacks variation
- one comma instead of a full stop (can you find it?)
- Not enough variation and precise description to move much beyond a C grade.

Answer 7

This is the opening of a long descriptive piece.

A brown carpet stretches before me, mud flecked, creased, and like boats tossed on a sea of dirty nylon are rows of desks. Children sit at these desks, heads down, scribbling furiously for fear that if they should remove their pens from the page they would drown. I know these people who write frantically, fearfully. These are my comrades soldiering their way through tasks sometimes beyond their young minds. If they should look up from their task to think, or to allow their minds to wander briefly for a moment, they would see mint green walls, chipped to reveal white plaster. Wooden slats surrounding the top of the room, reminiscent of a cage, keeping them trapped in this seemingly innocent room. A room which holds tortures beyond the imagination of those who suffered on the rack or endured the thumbscrews of the middle ages. Under the normal guise this room is not daunting, unless of course gym lessons are your idea of pain. Tied to the walls are tennis nets and basketball hoops surround the pupils in their sea of misery.

Examiner's comments:
- this engages the reader's interest from the start
- makes the reader think – what is the 'sea of nylon'?
- makes the reader imagine, too
- range of detailed description
- effective use of wide vocabulary
- variation of sentence structure throughout
- effective use of modifiers
- touch of humour in the gym lessons
- keeps the reader wondering what is coming next
- very accurate and controlled writing
- work of the highest standard – A*.